The 90-Minute Book

The Best Way To
Get All The Leads You Need

Dean Jackson

The 90-Minute Book

Printed by:
90-Minute Books
302 Martinique Drive
Winter Haven, FL 33884

www.90minutebooks.com

Copyright © 2013-2017, Dean Jackson

Published in the United States of America

131201-001.3

ISBN-13: 978-1947313965
ISBN-10: 1947313967

For more information on 90-Minute Books including
finding out how you can publish your own book, visit
90minutebooks.com or call (863) 318-0464

Here's What's Inside...

The 90-Minute Book!

Back in the summer of 2013, I arrived in London for a Breakthrough Blueprint Live event I was holding at the Tower Bridge Hotel.

Serendipitously, Dan Sullivan and Babs Smith, founders of Strategic Coach were in London at the same time.

We spent the day wandering around SoHo and the conversation turned to books.

Dan had just finished a book he wrote in just one day. He was excited about the potential of a new model of creating version 1 of a book, the first 80%, and not getting caught up in the endless cycle of planning and waiting till it's just right to get it out into the world.

This was like music to my ears.

I told Dan I would have my first book done and delivered to Strategic Coach in time for my next workshop in 2 weeks. I got that book done, and in the process, I got hooked on being able to write books at the speed of thought.

When Dan shared the distinction between being an author, not a writer, I realized the true focus should be on helping authors not get blocked by the process of writing.

Since then, we've put a team in place who have helped us produce over 300 books with a unique process we call "*The 90-Minute Book*".

This book is a result of that exact process.

The process works and we've helped many others easily and quickly get their first book out into the world using the 80% approach, where it's identifying invisible leads and generating new business.

This book was conceived, outlined, and written in less than 90-minutes of my time. I spent 30 minutes brainstorming the outline and 60 minutes recording the content. All in less than a 24-hour timeframe.

From there, the whole process was handled by the team put in place to make this process easy.

This is your chance to listen in as I describe the process and the benefits it can bring you.

Enjoy the book. I hope it changes the way you think about books and encourages you to take the leap and get your first book out into the world!

To your success.

Dean Jackson

Introduction

Susan: I'm excited to be able to speak with Dean Jackson today on what will be the inaugural 90-Minute Book. This is going to be a great process to share and opens up a whole new opportunity for business owners to reach new customers and clients.

So, having been attracted by the title, I guess the questions on reader's minds will be, 90-Minutes, is that really possible?

Dean: Here's the thing. This is a new concept, a new process for many, but I've been using it for a long time now and I've start to refer to it as 'The 90-Minute Book' because I've written several of these short books, that are a single concept to get a message out there. We've refined it and have it down to a process where the whole thing can happen in 90 minutes of my time.

This conversation is the perfect example of that in action. It's a single concept and started with the suggestion, "Why don't you come on here with me and we'll do a 90-minute book about 90-minute books?".

It feels a bit like Kramer, from Seinfeld, doing his coffee table book about coffee tables. A book about the book.

The general idea is that entrepreneurs, business owners, coaches, anyone who is in business that needs to be introduced to new people, can reach that audience through a book. This is especially easy if they remove all the unnecessary baggage that slow the process.

They have an idea rolling around in their head that they want to spread, and they can talk about it at length. They can share the idea. They want to spread it. They know their stuff, but they get blocked in getting it out there because they get intimidated by the thought of 'writing'.

Too many people don't go any further than just the thought "Someday I'd like to write a book".

Why Don't More People Write Books?

Susan: It's easy to imagine that person. I've even had that conversation with people myself. Is that why more people don't write books?

Dean: There are many different reasons. One of the ideas is it takes too long. People are intimidated by it. They have this process in mind that seems daunting. It seems like it's long hours of solitude in an unlit room and a candle and silence, sitting down and staring at that blank page. It's really intimidating.

Ultimately, most people don't like to write. It's the same thing when we go through school. Nobody likes to sit down and have to stare at a blank page and actually write something. People are often shy about their writings. They might not think they are good writers or they might be intimidated by making sure they have the right grammar or writing style, and the approach has to be just so.

All of those things, when you add them up, are a pretty good deterrent to writing a book. For every book that ends up being written, there are many more people walking around with the book in their head, and they never get it out into the world.

Susan: I think people literally don't know what format to write in. Even the thought of sitting down with an open Word document causes them to freeze and not go any further.

Dean: That's the thing. They haven't been trained in the concept of doing a good outline first, of brainstorming and getting all their thoughts out on paper, all the ideas they want to cover. This is the most valuable part of the process. It's the first part of the 90-Minute Book process; spending 30 minutes brainstorming and outlining to put a context around the message that you want to share so you can put your content within those subheads or categories.

This process of grouping your ideas together is usually fun for people once they know how to do it because it's bringing together the best part of your message.

Don't Focus on Being a "Writer"... Focus on Being an Author

Dan Sullivan said to me in one of our Strategic Coach workshops "You don't have to write to be an author". That's pretty profound. I realized **authorship is really about ownership of the idea** and it's about the creative process around the message. It's your idea. You're the author of the content.

But the writing doesn't have to be you. When you really think about it, all of the celebrity books you see, celebrities who write their memoirs or write about success or self-help books, they're not actually sitting down and writing these books in their writing room, with their typewriter.

They're speaking the book to a ghostwriter who they work with. That's why a lot of times you'll see the name of the celebrity is the big name, the author, and then it will say, 'with Susan Austin' or 'with Dean Jackson', whoever is the actual ghostwriter of that book.

The reality is the ghostwriter is the one who has done all the writing, but it's the authorship, the ideas that people are interested. It's about being interviewed and getting your idea out into a format where somebody can get it transcribed and turn it into a book.

I think you hit on an important point when you said people get caught up in really not knowing what to do which is a shame because that's just the logistics of it. They don't know where to start, but the logistics are simple for someone else to help with.

I can give you a process and talk you through a 30-minute interview to gather the information, what it is you want to share. Go through this with a skilled outliner and you've done a lot of content creation and a lot of program creation by the end of the process.

You can think contextually. You can put things into containers and create a path, a track to run on from the beginning to the end of your book.

I've done this many times now with the team here so it's easy for us to sit down and create an outline, a path to take you through this process, but even if you are reading this for the first time, it's something you can do too.

You Have an Important Message!

The other reason people don't write books is they don't think they could or should write a book! They don't understand why they would want to write a book. It may not be a burning desire to write a big life's work or to write what they would perceive to be a 250-300 page bookstore. But there are lots of reasons why it would be a good idea for you to write a book that gets that one idea out into the world, that one idea that people get value from and starts a conversation with somebody that you'd like to work with or you'd like to be in relationship with.

Any coach, entrepreneur, advisor, consultant or professional would have lots of reasons to write a book like that.

Once you understand this process is not about sitting in a room and writing, but that you could get the whole process done in 90 minutes and get an idea out there that starts a conversation, it becomes a great tool.

Now, you've got a book that you can use to generate leads. That's one of the best things. If you're doing advertising or speaking, and you've got a book that you can offer to people, it's a great way to start a conversation.

Susan: It takes all the feelings of being overwhelmed about writing a book and simplifies it into manageable steps.

Dean: That's right, one of the main reasons to do a 90-minute book, as opposed to writing a big masterwork, is that it's...

Susan: A 9-month book...

Dean: Right. It's that it is so much faster to get a 90-minute book out into the world with this process. You should be able to communicate the essence of your idea and add a lot of value in a one-hour conversation about it. It's enough time to really explore your idea, to get the main points out there in a way that start the conversation, gets buy-in on the idea, compels someone thot hake the next step or at least start them down a path and educations them on what your concept is.

The book you create allows you to get in front of people who you want to have that conversation with. I'll give some great examples of this as we go, but even starting this book as an example, it's started a conversation with you as you read it now.

No one reading this book, knew what the content was before they got to it, but if you're intrigued by the idea of creating a book in 90-minutes then it resonated with you and we've started a conversation.

How did we do that? We're doing it now by writing a 90-minute book to illustrate and explain the process of 90-minute books.

So this becomes a very useful tool, because otherwise, if you've got a service or product or a way that you can help people get a result, but don't have an easy way to start a conversation with them, you're forced to struggle, trying to find new people.

If you can get involved in a conversation they are already having and use a 90-minute book as a way to test a concept, you save time.

If I were to take 90 days to outline this idea, write a lot about the concept and the process, and then put it out there to the sound of crickets, I'd have invested a lot of time and a lot of effort into something that may not even be viable concept. It may not be something that the audience even wants.

Susan: You make a good point about the alternative and taking 90 days. One of the brilliances of this process is that it almost has to be simple which is more likely to resonate with readers. You could go on and on for days about why someone should write a book but it's just going to overwhelm them.

Whereas here, we're getting right into the meat of things because you only have an hour.

It's the most important points, the most valuable bits that someone can digest in one sitting and get to the end thinking, yes, I want to know more.

Dean: And I think that is what these 90-minute books are the best at.

Sharing a great idea as a way to start a conversation.

In the Breakthrough Blueprint program and on the I Love Marketing podcasts, we talk about this concept of the 3 units of your business: the before unit, the during unit, and the after unit; the before unit being the part of your business in charge of finding people who want to do whatever it is you do. If you're a coach, finding people who want to get the results you can coach them to get, if you're a real estate agent, finding people who want to buy and sell, if you're a financial advisor, finding people who want help managing their money.

You're using your book to get in front of the people who ultimately could be your ideal prospects, and do it in a way that speaks directly to them.

The thing about a 90-minute book and investing into that initial process is that it fits in with the idea of selecting a single target market because you can write a book that is specifically geared to that audience.

We have a gentleman in my mastermind group, John Smallwood, he's a financial advisor, and he has written now 3 books. He's used this 90-minute book concept to write a very specific book called *The Cosmetic Surgeon's Guide to Early Retirement*, specifically geared towards cosmetic surgeons. He's also written a broader book called *The Physician's Guide to Early Retirement*, which is a great fit for all physicians, and then a general book for everyone looking for financial advice, *5 Ways Your Wealth Is Under Attack*.

All 3 of these books are small, targeted, 90-minute books designed to start a conversation.

If you're going to use a book for lead generation, what I've really discovered is this concept of the minimum viable book is the best way to quickly, and cost effectively get your idea out to test with those that really matter. Your potential customers.

The Only 3 Things You Need to Get Your Ideas Out in the Marketplace

There are only three things you need to use a book as a lead generator. You have to have a book, so you can offer a book.

It doesn't matter whether the book is 40 pages or 240 pages, it just has to provide value. When people ask for it, they don't ask based on a page count, they ask based on the promise of getting an answer to a question.

So, the next thing you need is a title that gets your audience to say, "I want that."

If you're writing a book called *The Cosmetic Surgeon's Guide to Early Retirement*, and I'm a cosmetic surgeon who sees I can get a free book called *The Cosmetic Surgeon's Guide to Early Retirement*, I'm going to say, "I want that!". And that's done its job.

Now, you have to have a simple way to make people aware of your book. That's the third element.

Another gentleman in my mastermind group is Yuri Zolov. He wrote a 90-minute book called *Hypnotize Your Husband*.

This guy is an action-taker. He came to my Breakthrough Blueprint even in London and we talked about this concept. We came up with the name, "*Hypnotize Your Husband: How to Make Him Want You, Only You, And Never Even Look at Anybody Else.*" That was the essence of the book.

We drew out a little flyer concept that had a picture of the book cover, and the headline 'Free Book, *Hypnotize Your Husband: How to Make Him Want You, Only You, And Never Even Look at Anybody Else*, and go to HypnotizeYourHusband.com'. That's all the message needed to be.

When someone sees the ad they see it's a free book. They see the title, *Hypnotize Your Husband*, and the easy way to get a copy from HypnotizeYourHusband.com. There is no resistance, if they resonate with the title. The process is doing its job.

It doesn't matter whether the book is 40 pages or 240 pages, because you're not even mentioning that. It's not a selling benefit. It's not a benefit to get people interested, especially if you are giving away a copy as a way to start a conversation.

People get unnecessarily hung up on size.

The important thing is to package up a valuable message into a book that is useful to someone. An hours interview, just like we're doing now, tends to create a 40-50 in 5x8 paperback format. To me it's the perfect size. A 45-minute read someone can complete in one-sitting. Something you can take on the plane and read in one flight.

If you look at the statistics about book reading, most of the people who buy books never get past the first chapter. We're trying to do the opposite here. We're trying to give people the best introduction to your idea, and give them a way to learn more (the conversation).

People buy the book because they want the benefit that the title of the book promises. People buy *The 4-Hour Workweek*, a big book, or *The 4-Hour Body* by Tim Ferriss, because they want that promise. They want the benefit but they'll rarely get through the whole book.

Susan: Should someone always offer their book always free?

Dean: It doesn't have to be. But I think in this concept, it's the best way to start the conversation.

Sometimes people think, "Well, I'd rather write a big book and get a New York Times bestseller". They think that writing a book is going to put them on easy street, that they'll be able to retire off their royalties.

I know enough people who have written New York Times best sellers to know that that's not the truth. That's not the whole story. There's a lot more that goes into getting a book on the New York Times best-seller list than it may seem at first glance. People might think, "Well, if you just write a great book, that's going to rise to the top." But there's a lot more engineering, orchestrating and manipulating needed to get onto a bestseller list and it's a very expensive process.

There's a formula for it and it's certainly something you can do, but it takes money advice from people who know how to get there.

The far bigger opportunity for most people is not about creating a bestseller. It's about getting into a relationship, a conversation with more people who would benefit from their business.

If you take a coach or a consultant as an example, and take the 90-minute book approach to create a valuable book that introduces your idea and gives people meaningful action steps. Even if you give away this first part of your program (the part that becomes your book), you can create far more value by packaging the information you would put in the remaining 200 pages, were you to try to create the bigger book.

Packaging that content with audios and a workbook to sell for $199 instead of putting it all in a $19 book is going to give you far greater returns because the perceived value of a course is higher than the perceived value of a book.

Susan: You're not going to get someone to buy a $180 book. But people will sign up for a $180 course, especially after they have got value from your free book.

Dean: That's exactly right.

After they've read the book you've given them the best advice out there and you've got the best thing for them to do next.

Not only that, but for all those who are interested, but not interested today, you've still collected their details so you can continue the conversation until they are ready.

There are so many different ways for you to get your offer in front of people these days from the technically complicated to the most simple. Yuri, right now, has been putting out flyers on bus shelters and all over the city in Toronto, and generating leads of people who want to get the book. He has that drive, that hustle! After they get a copy of the book he invites them to come to a free workshop, where he'll invite them to a live event.

That whole process, knowing where you want people to go next, knowing what to do once you start that conversation is where the real, scalable leverage is.

Knowing you can help people understanding their perspective and knowing the best next step allows you to collect all the leads you need today because you know that some are ready today, but you'll also be there for those who are ready tomorrow.

Your book really is the best tool to turn what I call invisible prospects into visible prospects. If you have a book, now you can offer that to people who have no other reason to identify themselves and you'd have no access to or reason start a conversation with.

The advantage of really adopting this process and adopting it quickly is the access to a huge market that slower movers may miss. The investment is so low it give you a huge opportunity to test before committing more resources.

Even if you think about this type of book as version one of your book. It doesn't have to be the finished end product. The days of having to typeset things or have to commit to high volume print run, where you feel like you've got to proof the book and have everything perfect because you're going to be stuck with 5,000 or 10,000 copies are gone. Now, using digital, on-demand printing you can create smaller print runs down to individual copies. Services like Amazon's CreateSpace allow us to create this book very quickly and if we need to make changes later, there is no inventory to have to deal with.

Our typical 5x8 paperback books costs less than $2.50 to print, whether you're printing one or 1,000 of them.

The concept of creating the book quickly to test the market is a game changer.

Having your book out there is in every way better than waiting for things to be perfect and holding off from pulling the trigger.

How Dan Sullivan's 80% Approach Changed My View of What's Possible

About a year ago, as we record this, I was in London at the same time as Dan Sullivan and Babs Smith, founders of Strategic Coach. We ended up spending the day together. Dan was talking about his process of creating books using CreateSpace. He's the person who really introduced me to the concept. He shared with me how he had done the whole thing, writing it all in just one day so he had it ready for our next workshop, coming up in 2 weeks.

I looked at it and said, "Okay, I'm going to do that myself. I'm going to create a book, and I'm going to have 50 copies of it delivered to Strategic Coach before my workshop in 2 weeks.".

I used the process to create the *Breakthrough DNA* book. I outlined my thoughts, recorded it, had it transcribed, formatted, printed and delivered to Strategic Coach the day before my workshop.

That whole process, the first one I did took some time because I was laying the track as I went. But the next was faster, and the third faster, still as the team started to build on the knowledge they were gaining from each one.

Now I know this is a capability I have in my business. I can write books, 90-minute books, with only 90 minutes of my time involvement. I spend 30 minutes doing the outline, and then one hour recording.

I've been doing this for long enough that I could talk for an hour myself without any kind of interaction, which is exactly how I did the *Breakthrough DNA* book. But I realized that most people don't feel that way. They feel more comfortable having a conversation like we're having now. I also realized that talking through the idea with someone improves the conversation. I put more thought into it as I want you to understand the concept and you're there to kind of keep me on track through the process as well.

Susan: As opposed to someone who's going to get a recorder and just talk. Even if I don't say much, your thought process of having to articulate it so I understand it in a conversational, friendly manner is huge.

Dean: That's right, and checking in with you every now and then, to see if I'm making sense and you understand what we're saying.

Dan's idea of this being version one was so valuable because it freed me from so many of the concerns holding me back. In fact, I actually put "Version One: Send your ideas and feedback to Dean@DeanJackson.com," on the cover of *Breakthrough DNA*. It took away the resistance and allowed me to get the concept out there, get the conversation started, see what people say about it, how they interact with it, how they're using it, share their ideas, and if necessary update and integrate the feedback into version 2.

Susan: For the perfectionist listening, this is an easy way for them to deal with the fact that it doesn't have to be perfect. You can always refine your book but step one is the starting process to get it written.

Dean: I can't give Dan Sullivan enough credit for opening up my eyes to this. Of all the people he's shared this concept with, I think he'll admit, I've really taken it and run with it as much as you can, because I get it on a deep level.

He has a new book out called *The 80% Approach*, it's the idea that the first 80% is the biggest game changer. Going from having no book to having a book is a huge improvement. You've got a book you can use, you've got a title that resonates, and you've got the one-hour introduction to your idea out into the world.

That is the most valuable 80%, because you've gone from zero to 80%.

Now, if you were to spend more time and improve that by another 80%, you've only taken it to 96%. You've only gained a little bit more compared to the initial 80%. The return on the next 80% effort is smaller still because you're making smaller and smaller, incremental improvements.

That was a concept that I've always had in mind. When I look for breakthroughs in a business, I'm looking for things that you're not already doing. Any result you get is then usually an exponential improvement over what your result were, rather than taking an existing process that's working and spending a lot of time improving it to get incremental improvements. It's not the same. It's always better to look for the exponential improvement first, and get all of those out into the world.

The exponential opportunity here is realizing the first version of your book does not need to be the end product. You may continue to polish it, you may add to it, you may go on with it, but you may also realize that 80% is good enough. You may realize that it's enough to start the conversation, and that's all that matters. The greater opportunity is your next 80% market.

The 90-Minute Book Works for Lots of Different Businesses

Right now, in Success magazine, I have a full-page ad running that is written as an informative article and at the end offers a free copy of a book called *Email Mastery*. That book, written before I started using the 90-Minute Book process, is the transcript of 4 episodes of the I Love Marketing podcast I recorded with Joe Polish talking about email marketing. We had those transcribed and turned into the *Email Mastery* book.

The whole purpose of creating the books is to get it into the hands of people who are interested in email marketing and start a conversation. We've generated at this point almost 1,000 leads.

Remember I said one of the best ways to use a book is to identify invisible leads and engaging in a dialogue with those people to introduce them to other options. Now I know who they are I can talk with them and introduce them to the email mastery class, a $1,500 course that people can go through, a much more interactive program to help them get results using email, but it all started with the conversation offering this book called *Email Mastery*.

That's as easy as it can be. But even if you're marketing products, you can still use a book to start the conversation.

One of the people in my mastermind group is Luba Winter. She lives in Portland and has a company called NuWay Beauty. She created a device that combines ultrasound, galvanic waves, and red and blue LED lights in one handheld device that you can use at home. For 10 minutes a day, it penetrates your skin and stimulates your elastin and collagen. It has many benefits for example in anti-aging, it removes wrinkles, makes your skin plumper, cures loose skin, and makes you look younger, but one of the things that I was most excited about is that it cures acne.

The blue LED lights kill the bacteria that cause acne, and the red LED lights stimulate your own elastin and collagen. It's a process of curing the acne from the inside-out, going all the way down to the deepest levels of the skin and addressing the issue there, rather than just treating, topically, the symptoms of the acne, the end result. Rather than patching the leak, so to speak, you fix the roof.

It's a device that requires some education. If people saw it and you explained it, they wouldn't necessarily understand what it is. So, we created a book called *The Adult Acne Cure*, and advertise this book instead of advertising the device. The great news is the people who are going to download or request the book are people who have adult acne and that's exactly the person she wants to be in conversation with.

In the book, we can educate people on the causes of acne, the different types of acne, and then talk about the science behind the elements that are in the device Luba has to cure acne.

It talks about the scientific evidence of LED lights, ultrasonic waves, and the galvanic waves and outlines a treatment plan that now educates them about the process. And now, you can introduce them to the device that has all of those things they've read about in the book in one easy-to-use, at-home device.

You're starting the book with the end in mind. If you have a device that cures acne, you want to be in conversation with people who have acne, or their loved ones have acne. So having a book you can offer that is free and talks about the adult acne cure, is hugely valuable to help you identify people you want to engage.

Same thing with *The Cosmetic Surgeon's Guide to Early Retirement*. It's not book about, "Hey, let me show you how I can work with your financial plan", it's about getting a useful message out to cosmetic surgeons about early retirement.

Same kind of thing with Yuri's book, *Hypnotize Your Husband*. Yuri is a clinical hypnotherapist so ultimately there are lots of ways he can help people.

Rather than focusing on losing weight or stopping smoking or reducing stress; the big 3 area's in hypnosis but a very competitive, having a side door to identify people who are open to hypnosis generally is a great tool.

This particular title is also interesting to consider because it's almost like 'hypnotize your husband' is the only socially acceptable option for a title. It wouldn't be the same reaction if there were a book called 'Hypnotize Your Wife'. That has a whole different vibe. 'Hypnotize Your Kids', or 'Hypnotize Your Mother-In-Law'. Those kinds of things sound like titles people would be up in arms about that.

But *Hypnotize Your Husband* sounds sort of funny. It creates a curiosity around it. It starts the conversation about hypnosis.

If you can show someone benefits in one area, they are more likely to be interested in other related solutions. Yuri's a very skilled hypnotist and he can show people how to use hypnotic principles in conversation. How you can use conversational hypnosis, suggestion, to get your husband to be more romantic or to buy you flowers, or to take out the garbage, or to do whatever it is that you'd want to hypnotize your husband to do.

As people see success in that area, now they're open to hypnosis and think "Wow, I didn't know hypnosis could do this." They see the world of possibilities that hypnosis could open up, all because you started a conversation in a lighthearted way with someone who had an interest in hypnotizing their husband.

How a 90-Minute Book Can Help You Get More Clients and Make More Sales

Susan: I'm curious about Luba's market. How is she finding success with the concept of writing a book to sell a product?

Dean: It's useful to see the book in the context of the 8-profit activators in the Breakthrough DNA process I mentioned. These 8 individual stages fit into either the Before, During or After unit of your business. Your book is a great tool to identify leads for your Before unit ('Before' people are doing business with you).

So, in the before unit, the profit activators are:

- **Profit Activator 1**
  Narrow your focus and select ONE single target market (at a time).

- **Profit Activator 2**
  Use direct response to compel prospects to call you or raise their hand.

- **Profit Activator 3**
  Patiently and systematically educate and motivate prospects to meet you… when they are ready

- **Profit Activator 4**
  Present your unique service offer in a way that makes it easy to get started.

Let's walk through this.

Often, when you have a product or service that can help many different people, like Luba's device that could help all people with skin, anywhere in the world, look better and feel younger, people want to cast a wide net to identify leads. They don't want to leave anyone out.

But, the very best thing you can do is select a single target market for your effort to attract leads. You're not going to turn away other business, but your effort should be focused.

One of the most transformational experiences Luba saw with customers is curing acne. Having the end in mind & know we want people to buy the device, let's narrow that further to choose people with adult acne. They are more likely to have the disposable income to turn into paying customers.

Adult acne is different as a target market than teen acne, but if you identify a parent who has adult acne, and they see how this works and understand that it will work for their kids, then you've got an entry into that market too.

We choose a single target market, adult acne, we even added a geographic constraint. Luba lives in Portland, so we've decided let's just start with adult acne in Portland to test the idea.

The last step is to find people in the ideal target audience and get them involved in the conversation.

You can't buy a list of people with adult acne or someone who's just had a breakout or is concerned about their adult acne. You need to get them to raise their hand in another way so you can communicate with them.

Offering a book using pay per click ads, Facebook ads, flyers, business cards or magazine ads, lead generators that use the title "Free Book: *The Adult Acne Cure*. Visit TheAdultAcneCure.com to get your copy" is how we reach people in Profit Activator 2 and get them to raise their hand.

So now we've selected a target market. We've got them to come and raise their hand. The book itself is going to do a lot of the work of educating them and give them the information they need to understand the Rejuvenation G4 is the device that can help them get the results they want.

It will educate them on how acne is created, and show the layers of the skin, where it starts in the pores, and how it manifests. Then it will talk about the scientific of how blue LED light kills the bacteria in the deeper layers of the skin that cause the acne, and the red LED light stimulates collagen and elastin, which are the things that make your skin look healthy, plump, tight and smooth. The kinds of things that stimulate new growth of the cells below the surface that now come out as healthy skin. And lastly how, in 60 or 90 days, someone can be completely cured of their acne and have incredible, beautiful-looking skin.

That's the education process. We show them how it works, how it works for them and then make an offer in Profit Activator 4.

This is the purpose of your book. To start a conversation so you're in a dialogue with an interested person. Now you can really help people along the process of getting the benefit they identified they want by being attracted to the title of the book you offered.

You grab the attention of your target audience by offering a book called *The Adult Acne Cure*, knowing what they really want is they want the cure. When you educate them, they understand why nothing they're doing on top of their skin is a long-term solution and they've got to go deeper to really create the cure.

Then, knowing the device works, she has set up a Bill Me Later service with PayPal, to create a situation where she can invite people to go through the process, to try the device with all the skincare products for 60 days, to go through the whole process, and it will either cure your adult acne or it won't. If it doesn't, you won't have paid anything. If it does, then you can keep the device, and you've got up to 6 months to pay because you've used the Bill Me Later function.

That's crafting an irresistible offer in Profit Activator 4. You're either going to cure your acne, in which case it's 100% worth going through the process, or you're going to try it and it's not going to work, which is maybe 5% of the people because their compliance of doing the actual treatments isn't consistent, in which case they can send it back and not have spent any money to try it.

It's such a great, compelling funnel at every stage and it educational to see how it works from target audience, to book to sales.

Susan: So different from most people who are just trying to sell in their ad. They would just come out and try to sell the device. There wouldn't be any education.

Dean: You're absolutely right and it's all focused on them and their product not the customer.

This format we're discussing right here is ultimately the very best example of it too.

Anybody reading this book right now who's read this far is the perfect candidate to create a 90-Minute Book. They were attracted to the title because they have the idea a book would be valuable to their business, but they don't know they could or how they could do it in 90 minutes. It sounds attractive. 'I've got 90 minutes, and I'd love to have a book'.

Now we've explained, we've educated people about the process, about how it works, and about many different ways you can use a book. They just need to come up with a title that their audience would say, "I want that!"

When I was in London, we spent a lot of time on different book titles at the Breakthrough

Blueprint event. We have a gentleman who does corporate training for businesses, on productivity, so he wrote a book called *The Fire-Free Workday*.

Just hearing that title, that sounds like, "Wow, if I could just be uninterrupted, I could get a lot of stuff done." That's attractive.

We had a gentleman wrote *The Influential Introvert: How to Get Your Voice Heard at Home, at Work, and with Your Friends*. For someone who's an introvert, they can feel like they don't get heard. It's even harder to feel influential but this is a solution to that.

I helped a fitness guru who owns a gym, a training studio in Ireland write a book called *The Skinny Jean Solution*.

All these titles resonate with their target markets. Someone hears the title and they want the thing that's promised. That's the real reason people buy books, because we're buying the hope that ownership of that book is going to give us the result that the book promises. That's why we buy that book, that process, and that's why they are so powerful at getting people to raise their hands.

Here's Exactly How the 90-Minute Book System Works

The process we're going through here, the one we're using to create a book called *The 90-Minute Book* is the exact same system we use for others.

We took 30 minutes to outline the process, the important point of creating a book and its purpose, and we've spent almost 60 minutes recording. All that's left is the final production stage.

When we're done it will automatically go to our Production team who will facilitate the whole process of getting it transcribed, and then taking that transcript checking it for spelling or grammatical errors and putting it into our book layout format including titles, chapter, table of content. Our Design team will start creating a cover for the book that really makes it stand out and run that past me. They'll upload it, get copies printed and delivered to me, and I won't have spent any more time than the 90 minutes I've illustrated here today.

It's the perfect proof of the 90-minute book concept at work.

The last book that I created like this was called *The Self Milking Cow*. In that book, I outlined the idea that there are 2 types of people: there are cows and there are farmers. Cows being the idea people, the entrepreneurs, the creators, the people who want to get their ideas out into the world. Kind of like a cash cow world, and the only thing standing in their way is setting up a process that lets some helpful Farmers help them with the process. It's very difficult for Cows to milk themselves, because they need opposable thumbs.

It's painful and frustrating if you're trying to be a self-milking cow but most of them have no problem with getting the ideas out there. They're ready to talk at length and in detail about their ideas and about their concepts. If only they had a reliable way to get those ideas out.

That's what we've set up. A group of Farmers to helpfully guide you through the milking shed. To help you dial in a title that resonates. To keep it all on-track with an outline that has a beginning, a middle and an end. To capture the information in a friendly, comfortable, 60-minutes recording. To have professionals designers create a killer cover and to pull it all together and take care of the many other Production issues that would drive most Cows back out to the pasture.

As a happy Cow myself, I'm spreading the word about my Farmers who are ready and able to help me get my ideas out into the world, so I can just spend refining my ideas and then move on to the next book.

It is a game changer and a way to 10x your productivity and the value you share with your customers.

Susan: So to clarify the process we have created for someone that's interested in doing their own 90-minute book... They would take 30-minutes to work on the outline with us and then 60-minutes to capture their content in just the same way we've done today, but all those other things you mentioned, the transcription, the formatting, the cover designs, the team handles all those details. They don't have to do anything, except the call.

Dean: Absolutely. Because that's the farm work. That's the work that requires opposable thumbs. It's the technical work that most people get blocked with.

Even if they get on board with the concept of "Well, I could see myself doing this book," but then, "How do I format it? Where do I get them printed? How do I get that set up? How do you design the cover? What are the dimensions? Do I need a designer? How can I get it transcribed? How can I get that all put together?" There are so many 'how' questions that people have that stop them from taking action.

What I've really discovered is that the best question Cows can ask is not, "How do I do something?" The best question is, "Who can do something?"

It's always better to ask "What do I want?" and focus on, "What do I want to say? What do I want to share? What's the name of my book? What's the most valuable information I know?" and then ask the question, "Who can do that for me? Who can get this out into the world?" rather than how do I get that out there?"

It's so much faster when you have the right "who" so you can say "That was easy!"

After a year of doing these, I just feel empowered. I think I've personally created 28 books now using this process and having the capability that anytime I want, I can spend 30 minutes to outline a book, do a 60-minute interview to capture it and have all the rest of it completely done for me, that's an incredible capability.

Susan: This is life changing for a lot of business owners who have amazing information to engage potential customers, but are stuck with the ideas in their head that they don't know how to get out into the world.

Dean: I'm very excited about it. We have 90MinuteBooks.com as the home for doing this process for people, and taking what I've learnt from creating courses like "*How to Write, Publish and Sell a Moneymaking Book.*" and having personally created many books, we're waiting to help people pick great titles, understand what kinds of books are most compelling and the concept of creating a great outline.

Anyone who goes through the process will start in just the same way we did to create this book. A 30-minute conversation to get the outline together, and then a 60-minute recording to capture their ideas and bring out their best thinking, and they're done. Their whole book could be completed and delivered to them without them having to use their opposable thumbs at all. It's Happy Cow Approved.

Susan: The cows of the world thank you!

As I've been talking to the people we've initially been working with, that has been the stand out theme. People have been so relieved to have finally got a straight forward way to capture their thoughts and get them on to the page in a way that is accessible for potential customers without creating a whole other job for them to do.

To be able to create an asset, an over time many assets, that can be out there, working to engage with new people.

Dean: I can't wait to see what comes of this, and to see all of the books that we're able to get out into the world using this process.

This has been fantastic. We've spent just over an hour right now going through the whole concept. I think this is a perfect example of how this process works.

We had a text exchange yesterday when I had the idea I wanted to do this book. We set up a 30-minute conversation yesterday to outline and the time for this call today to record and literally, that's it. That's my entire involvement in the process and here we have a 90-minute book that is living proof of the 90-Minute Books process working.

Thank you so much for helping, Susan. It's going to be a very exciting process to work with all kinds of people, getting their books out into the world.

Susan: Absolutely. A service that is much needed.

What to do next...

Here's How to Get Your First Book Outlined, Written and Published in Just 90-Minutes...

You already know what your book is about. You've spent years thinking about it and developing your specialized knowledge. The hard part is to get what's in your head out on paper where it can start spreading your idea.

That's where we come in. We help people just like you get your first book outlined, written and published in as little as 90 minutes.

> **Step 1**: We spend 30 minutes outlining and developing your chapters, titles, headlines, and questions to fully express your idea.
>
> **Step 2**: We record a 60-minute podcast style audio interview where you get to talk about your ideas in a comfortable format drawing out your best thinking.
>
> **Step 3**: We take it from there and get your call transcribed and formatted, create your cover and take all the steps to get your book printed and in your hands, just like this one.

Most people think it takes months of hard work and hours of writing in solitude to create a book.

Now you can get your book outlined, written and out in the world in just 90-minutes of your time.

If you'd like us to help, just send an email to: **hello@90minutebooks.com** and we'll take it from there.

Made in the USA
Columbia, SC
05 October 2020